# FAITH and LIFE

Twelve easy-to-use
housegroup studies

PAUL SMITH

*HEADLINE SPECIAL*

© 2002 Copyright Headway

All rights reserved.
No part of this publication may be reproduced, stored in a retrieval system, or transmitted, in any form or by any means, electronic, mechanical, photocopying, recording or otherwise, without the prior written permission of the publisher.

British Library Cataloguing in Publication Data.
A catalogue record for this book is available from the British Library

ISBN 978 0 86071 562 7

are published for Headway by

tel: 0115 932 0643 web: www.moorleys.co.uk

# FAITH AND LIFE

## Contents

| | | |
|---|---|---|
| 1. | What's God like? | 5 |
| 2. | Who are you? | 9 |
| 3. | Who is Jesus? | 13 |
| 4. | Who is the Holy Spirit? | 16 |
| 5. | What is the Church? | 19 |
| 6. | The life of prayer | 23 |
| 7. | What is worship? | 27 |
| 8. | Called as a witness | 30 |
| 9. | Life in the Spirit | 35 |
| 10. | Called to simplicity | 39 |
| 11. | Jesus' attitude to others | 42 |
| 12. | Jesus and his enemies | 45 |

# 1. What's God like?

## What's your picture of God?
Sometimes children at school are asked to draw a picture of God. If you have any teachers in your group they may be able to share some personal memories of the pictures resulting from such an exercise. Not surprisingly, the children find it difficult. Often an 'old man in the clouds' is the result.

Christians often use familiar biblical words to describe God. They are a kind of shorthand. We sometimes become so familiar with them that we forget what they really mean. Let's try to get behind the words to a real understanding of God. Take a moment to think about how you would describe God, and then share your descriptions. Try to avoid familiar or biblical words. Imagine you are trying to describe God to someone with no knowledge of the Bible.

## God in the Old Testament
The attitude people have towards God and especially the name they give him tells us a lot about what they believe about him.
You will need a Bible for this bit. We are going to look up some Old Testament passages which use different names for God. Look them up one at a time and after each one ask *'What picture or image of God does this name convey?'* Share your observations as you work through the list.

### Exodus 3:1-6, 13-15
How many names for God are here? What does each one tell us about him?

### Isaiah 6:1-4
What does this tell us about God?

### Deuteronomy 32:3&4, 39
Remember that it's people's experience of God that shapes the way they describe him.

### Ezekiel
Almost all his prophecies begin with, or contain, the words 'This is what the Sovereign Lord says...' You can thumb through the book and see how many you can find! What does this title tell us about the way that Ezekiel thought about God?

## What's in a name?
Does it really matter what we call God?

In biblical times a person's name had particular significance. It was not just what they were called. It was meant to convey something of the person's nature or character. Something of this is still with us. Most of us have, in our minds, a picture of the kind of character which ought to go with a particular name. Sometimes we meet people whose name and character do not seem to fit. 'She's not a Mildred', we say.

In **Genesis 32:22-32** we see Jacob wresting all night with a mysterious stranger. The demand to know his name was expressing a desire to know his nature. We must understand **John 14:14** and similar verses in this way. To ask in the name of Jesus is to ask according to his nature or character. The biblical names for God tell us a lot about how people thought about him.

## How did Jesus speak about God?
It is clear from the Gospels that Jesus stood in a unique, personal relationship with God. He spoke of God in a new way which demanded a revolution in people's thinking. By the time he was twelve years old he was referring to God as his Father (Luke 2:49). When he prayed he called God 'Father' (Luke 10:21). A quick scan through any of the Gospels reveals that Jesus saw himself in a most intimate relationship with God. It was this one thing, more than any other, which led to the conspiracy that resulted in his death (John 5:18).

Further, in his teaching Jesus spoke of God as the Father of the ordinary people who were listening to him speak (Luke 11:13, 12:30,32). When his disciples asked him to teach them to pray he told them to say 'Our Father...' (Matt 6:9).

*Was Jesus suggesting that everyone could have the same kind of relationship with God which he had?*

It is clear that the way in which Jesus spoke of God as 'Father' set the tone for the rest of the New Testament writers. Paul clearly sees this kind of relationship with God as a possibility for every Christian (Romans 8:15&16).

## Facing the problems
To speak of God as 'Father' in a 21st century Western culture is not without its difficulties. For some the problem is that 'father' is a male term. Others have suffered bad relationships with their natural fathers and so their concept of fatherhood is damaged. There is always the danger of losing a sense of the holiness and majesty of God, even becoming 'chummy' with him.

*Are these problems real for members of the group? If they are not real for us personally, how sensitive do we need to be to others within the local church?*
*To what extent should we modify our language in order to avoid causing hurt to others?*

## You and him - and them!

When Jesus taught his followers to pray 'Our Father...' he was indicating not only a new kind of relationship with God, but also a new kind of relationship between the disciples. The Lord's Prayer is all in the plural - us and our, not me and mine. When individuals from all sorts of backgrounds and cultures know God as Father it establishes a new relationship between them. If God is our Father, then we are siblings; so don't let's feel embarrassed about calling each other 'brother' and 'sister', for that is what God has made us.

### *Some questions to consider (if you have time)*

1. Do you think of God primarily as awesome, to be revered, or approachable, offering his friendship?

2. The balance between God's holiness and approachability is a delicate one. How do we preserve this balance in our private devotions and public worship?

3. The Bible has other pictures or metaphors for God. Can you think of any which you have found particularly helpful? You may want to make a list of the various titles that the biblical writers give to God. Psalm 23 may be a good starting point.

# 2. Who are You?

At a recent house-warming party, given by the people who had moved in next door to the manse, a stranger asked the minister, 'Who are you?'. He could have replied in a number of ways: 'I'm so-and-so' giving his name, 'I'm the minister of the Methodist Church', 'I'm the husband of Margaret'. But the person who asked the question would not have been any wiser! Instead, he quite naturally offered a reply in the context which she would understand: 'I'm the man from next door.'

We can all describe ourselves and each other in a variety of different ways. People can be described in terms of **physical appearance** - tall, short, thin, fat, colour of hair, colour of eyes, distinguishing features.

We also describe people in terms of **relationships** - so-and-so's wife, husband, child, parent, cousin.

Or we can describe people in terms of their **personality** - introvert, extrovert, selfish, kind, arrogant or loving.

Another way of describing people is to speak in **spiritual** terms - the kind of relationship we have with God and the way we practise that relationship.

## *A simple exercise*

Within your group each person should try to describe themselves using the four categories which we have just outlined - physical appearance, relationships, personality and spirituality. It would then be good if other members of the group were to add anything which they see in others but which they omitted when describing themselves. Try to be kind to each other!

These are not the only ways we describe ourselves and each other. Sometimes, for example, we would want to make reference to a person's job or profession. The categories which we use often depend on the context and the person to whom we are speaking; but they do provide points of reference which help us to feel secure. When these points of reference change it has a profound effect on us. We feel insecure. Others say, 'He's not the person he was' because who we are depends on the reference points by which we are defined.

*Can you think of people who have suffered a physical change which has resulted in a change in the way they perceive who they really are?*
*Can you think of examples where the change has been in their relationships, personality, or spirituality with a similar result?*

## *What does the Bible say?*
When the biblical writers describe human beings they are far more concerned with spiritual things than material things. We know a lot about Jesus, yet no biblical writer felt that it was important to tell us what he looked like! But they describe him so clearly in other ways that we feel we can get to know him. This is typical of the way the Bible talks about people. They are described, usually, in terms of their relationship to God and to the rest of creation, including other people. So what *does* the Bible say about human beings?

*We are going to make some observations and give some Bible references. Look them up as you work through the list. Pause after each one so that members of the group can reflect, share their insights and answer any questions.*

## All people are essentially equal in the sight of God.
In the early Old Testament period the Jewish nation was so convinced that they were the chosen people of God that they thought Gentiles were of far less worth to God. Later some of the prophets realised that God had chosen the Jews to be the channel through which his love would reach everyone, so all were of equal worth (Isa 49:1,6&7).

The ministry of Jesus demonstrated God's gracious love for everyone. Gentile kings were amongst the first to worship him (Matt 2:1-12). He healed a Roman officer's servant and commended the Roman's faith (Matt 8:5-13). He speaks of everyone being judged by the same criteria (Matt 25:31-46). His love is for the whole world (John 3:16).

We see clearly from Acts and Paul's letters that the members of the Early Church were convinced that the Christian gospel was for everyone.

*Can you think of scripture verses which use words like 'all', 'whoever', or 'anyone'? What are the implications of this for society, the church, and our own individual lives?*

## People are both body and soul
Sometimes we get confused by the words 'soul' and 'spirit'. We need to remember that the Bible uses these words interchangeably. Man is described as body and soul in Matt 6:25 and 10:28, and body and spirit in Eccles 12:7 and 1 Cor 5:3,5. Death is sometimes described as giving up the soul (Gen 35:18) and sometimes as giving up the spirit (Luke 23:46).

Our self-awareness confirms the scripture. Man is both physical and spiritual. *How would you define the soul or spirit?*

## People are made in the image of God
The creation story of Genesis 1 reaches its height when human beings are created. They are to be stewards of God's creation. They are created by him and resemble him (Gen 1:26&27). Clearly this cannot mean that they are made in his physical image, for God is spirit. Human beings are distinct from the rest of creation and bear the likeness of their creator. Their likeness to God concerns the spiritual dimension of their life. Like their creator, men and women have a moral awareness, a spiritual consciousness, the power of reason, immortality, freedom, the capacity to give and receive love.

*It may be easier to see the image of God in some people then others, but is it there in everyone?*

## People are sinners
If we are made in the image of God, clearly something has gone wrong. The Bible usually describes this by saying that people are sinners. It is a kind of shorthand way of recognising that they are not as God originally intended them to be. 'Sinners' may not be a popular word today, but it is the word which the Bible uses to describe people in their natural state. It is essentially descriptive of a broken relationship with God. By nature everyone wants their own way. However we understand the story in Gen 3:1-13 it is essentially about man choosing to do as he pleases and not to live as God requires. It is the story of every individual's life.

*What do you think about the statement 'We are not sinners because we sin; we sin because we are sinners'?*

## People live in tension
If we are both made in the image of God and, at the same time, sinners it is not surprising that we live with tension. The human race is conscious of its dignity and yet its insignificance (Ps.8). People have the potential for great good and great evil. We may strive to be better people, yet we are conscious of other influences which shape our personality and affect our decisions.

*Read Romans 7:14-25. There may be some things here which you do not understand, but in what ways do you identify with the tension which Paul felt?*

## People are made to have fellowship with God
Before man was disobedient he clearly had a perfect relationship with his Creator. After that act of disobedience this relationship was damaged, if not completely broken, and the rest of the Bible contains the story of God's gracious search for humanity, in order that the fellowship may be renewed. There is also a similar longing deep within the human heart. It is often

obscured by other things but men and women long for fellowship with their maker. Psalm 42:1&2 expresses the deepest longings of the human heart.

*Our longing for God often comes to the surface in times of crisis. Can you think of examples from your own life or the lives of others where this has been true?*

## People can be changed

Through the life, ministry, death and resurrection of Jesus a damaged relationship with God can be restored. Because human life finds meaning through its relationships with others, and because our relationship with God is fundamental, people are fundamentally changed when they begin a new relationship with God. That is why the Bible speaks of them as being new people - read 2 Cor 5:16-21. It is within this relationship that people can find their personal identity and a security, which is stronger than circumstances, crises, or even death.

*The Christian cannot answer the question 'Who are you?' without making reference to Christ. How would you answer that question?*

# 3. Who is Jesus?

The person of Jesus of Nazareth is central to the Christian faith. Everything which Christians believe comes from their understanding of who Jesus is and what he has done. His life is the point of reference for all Christian doctrine, practice, and ethics. His life, teaching, example, death and resurrection are fundamental.

*Spend some time sharing together what you believe about Jesus.*
It would be good to list the facts about which every member of your group is already convinced. Did he ever really exist? What can we know about his life? Are the things which we read about him in the Gospels reliable? Are there things about Jesus which we find it difficult to believe?
*Spend some time sharing your answers together.*

## What about the evidence?
There can be no doubt that there was an historic character called Jesus of Nazareth. Both biblical writers and other contemporary historians bear witness to the fact. There is more evidence for the existence of Jesus than there is for many other historical characters whose existence is never doubted: Julius Caesar, Cleopatra, William the Conqueror.

Josephus, a contemporary Jewish historian, writes about him thus:

> *'Now, there was about this time, Jesus, a wise man, if it be lawful to call him a man, for he was a doer of wonderful works - a teacher of such men as receive the truth with pleasure. He drew over to him both many of the Jews, and many of the Gentiles. He was [the] Christ; and when Pilate, at the suggestion of the principal men amongst us, had condemned him to the cross [AD 33, April 3], those who loved him at first did not forsake him, for he appeared to them alive again the third day [AD 33, April 5], and the divine prophets had foretold these and ten thousand other wonderful things concerning him; and the tribe of Christians, so named from him, are not extinct at this day.'*
> (Antiquities of the Jews, Book 18, chapter 3, para 3)

We must admit that most of the detailed evidence which we have is to be found in the Gospels. Mark was probably the first Gospel to be written. It was produced as a 'tract' - a simple document to put into the hands of people who wanted a pocket history about Jesus. Matthew and Luke probably came next. They took much of the information which Mark had provided and supplemented it with more detail. Matthew had certainly been an eye-witness of many of the events contained within his book. Luke was a doctor who became a Christian and was anxious to place before his readers reliable evidence which would stand the test of their scrutiny. He was a meticulous historian. John, who wrote in a different style, was also an eyewitness.

The level of evidence required to establish historical fact is often debated. We must be clear that there is far more evidence, written by people who witnessed the events, about the life of Jesus than about many other historical events and characters, yet we do not doubt the evidence about them. When we consider the evidence about Jesus we must be careful not to adopt a double standard, requiring a higher level of evidence for him than we would for any other character who lived about the same time.

*Take a look at the Gospels*
**Matthew 1:1** speaks of a 'record'; verse 18 begins to tell the story.
**Mark** begins his Gospel with a great announcement in which he gives a clue about who Jesus really was.

**Luke** in the first four verses of his Gospel places his credentials as an historian before the reader. He wants them to be sure of the reliability of the evidence he is going to bring.

**John** goes straight into the story. He wants the reader to read the story first. But before the story ends he makes it clear why he has written and how reliable his evidence is. Look at John 20:30&31 and John 21:24&25.

For twenty centuries the Gospels have stood more examination than any other piece of literature. They have stood the test. When we read the story which is recorded by Matthew, Mark, Luke and John we can be sure that we are reading historical fact.

## What others said about him
Maybe the life of Jesus has come under more scrutiny than any other because the claims which are made for him are unlike any other. Christians believe that this one life is unique. In order to come to a clear judgement about Jesus we must try to face the issues, not from where we stand, but from the perspective of those who first met, saw and heard him. As we read the Gospel story we discover that the question of who Jesus really is is placed firmly on the agenda of all who encountered him. Not surprisingly, we meet with a number of different reactions.

*Take a look at some passages in the Gospels to see what people said about him.*

**John 10:14-21** Look especially at verse 20. Why do you think they reacted like this to Jesus?

**John 7:1-13** What reactions do you see here? Notice how the personality of Jesus was making people formulate an opinion about him.

**Matthew 16:13-20** In this famous passage Jesus introduces the issue. He knew what his disciples were going to face and it was important for them to have a clear judgement about him. Look at verse 16. Peter, for the first time, puts into words what many had come to suspect: Jesus was more than just a good man.

**John 20:24-31** Thomas eventually had the evidence which he had been seeking, and so he was able to reach his own conclusion (v.28).

*Of the various reactions which we have just identified which do you think sums up the opinion of most people today? Which sums up your opinion? Is Thomas' reaction of a different kind from the rest?*

## What Jesus said about himself

The claims which Jesus made for himself are quite remarkable. Because we are so familiar with them we take them for granted. But if we try to see things through the eyes of those who saw him we can begin to discover what an impact he made. He accepted Peter's acknowledgement that he was the Messiah (Matt16:17-20). He accepted Thomas' worship (John 20:28&29).

*Take a look at some of the claims which Jesus made for himself which are recorded in St John's Gospel:*
John 10:7-10, 14-18; John 14:5-14; John 15:1-17
*Can you think of other passages in which Jesus makes a claim about himself?*

For we who are Christians and who acknowledge the unique place which Jesus occupies these statements are the subject of wonder and devotion. For those who first heard them, and for unbelievers today they are a scandal. What kind of person makes these claims for himself?

There are really only three alternatives:

1. He was mentally deranged. He had delusions of grandeur. We must not blame him, because he could not help it. But we can pity him and feel sorry that he came to such a sticky end.

2. He was a confidence trickster. His ego depended on his popularity and he discovered that the more remarkable his claims the more people believed him! It all went terribly wrong. When he died he got what he deserved.

3. What he said was true! He really is the person that his first followers believed him to be. The claims, which he made for himself, are an accurate portrayal of his true identity.

*Which of these alternatives represents your position? Share with other members of the group how your own under understanding of Jesus, and your attitude to him, has changed over the years.*

# 4. Who is the Holy Spirit?

Many Christians have difficulty in speaking about the Holy Spirit. The Bible gives us a picture of God as Father and Jesus as Son, but the images which the Bible gives for the Holy Spirit are difficult to imagine.

**Spend a moment sharing together some of the ways in which the Bible describes the Holy Spirit.**

Whilst many of us have difficulties in thinking about the Holy Spirit we cannot deny that the denominations and 'new churches' which place a particular emphasis on the Holy Spirit are the fastest growing branch of the church. They are also the branch which makes many traditional Christians feel uneasy.

**Share together any difficulties and unease which you personally may have in thinking or speaking about the Holy Spirit.**

It is quite clear that there is much confusion and not a little ignorance about the person and work of the Holy Spirit. We need to examine the Bible again to get our thinking straight.

## 1. The Bible speaks of the Holy Spirit as a Person
Look at John 15:26, John 16:7&8, Eph 4:30. Notice that the Holy Spirit is called 'he' not 'it'. We cannot grieve things, only people. The Holy Spirit is not a thing; he is a Person. This is important because it means that the Holy Spirit is One with whom we can have a relationship. We cannot have a relationship with things, only people.

## 2. The Bible speaks of the Holy Spirit as God
Look at Acts 5:3&4. The Holy Spirit is God's Spirit. That's why Christians affirm that God is Father, Son and Holy Spirit.

## 3. There is a variety of different titles for the Holy Spirit
Sometimes he is called the Spirit of God, sometimes the Spirit of Jesus, sometimes the Holy Spirit, sometimes the Spirit of truth, sometimes the Counsellor, and so on. It is really important that we don't get bogged down with the doctrine of the Trinity. If the Christian faith is primarily about a relationship with God this may be a helpful way of thinking about the Trinity. God the Father is Creator - God above us. Jesus is the Redeemer - God beside us. The Holy Spirit is the Enabler - God within us.

Ask yourself 'How can we know God today?' We may be aware of God as Creator, for we see his handiwork all around us; we may be aware of Jesus the

Redeemer, for we read his story in the Bible; but if we are to have a living experience of God today it will be God the Holy Spirit whom we encounter.

*Take a moment to think about occasions when you have been aware of the presence of God. Share with the rest of the group your experiences of meeting with God today.*

## 4. What does the Holy Spirit do?

So far we have tried to answer the question 'Who is the Holy Spirit?' Now we must discover what the Holy Spirit does. Once again we rely on the Bible as our source book. Take a look at the following verses and make a note of what the Holy Spirit is doing alongside each one:

> Genesis 1:2&3
>
> Exodus 31:1-5 (if you are using the GNB look at the footnote!)
>
> Numbers 11:24-30
>
> Numbers 24:1-3
>
> 2 Chronicles 15:1
>
> Ezekiel 2:1&2
>
> Joel 2:28&29
>
> John 1:29-34
>
> Acts 1:4&5
>
> Acts 2:38&39

The Holy Spirit of God, active at creation, enabling different people to fulfil the ministry which God gave to them, present in the life and ministry of Jesus, has been given to every Christian believer. Jesus promised that the Holy Spirit would dwell within every disciple (John 14:16&17), he would enable us to see the truth clearly and point us to Christ (John 16:12-15) and he would bring power (Acts 1:8).

## 5. The Holy Spirit's ministry is to make us more like Jesus
Look at Galatians 5:22-23

The qualities listed here are all descriptive of the character of Jesus. Yet they are spoken of as being the 'fruit' of the Spirit; the result of the Holy Spirit indwelling the Christian's life. It is the Holy Spirit's task to make us more like Jesus. This spiritual transformation of our character is not brought about by trying harder but by surrendering our lives entirely to God, so that his Spirit can fill us.

*How far does that statement agree with your own experience?*

## 6. The Holy Spirit gives gifts to every Christian
In the New Testament there are several lists of the 'gifts of the Holy Spirit'. Below you will find the references to two such lists. The group could split into two at this stage with one half taking each list.

*Look up the two lists in Romans 12:6-9 and 1 Corinthians 12:1-11 and list the gifts of the Spirit mentioned in them. How do we interpret them for today?*

We have not only learned that there are a variety of different gifts listed in the New Testament. We have also learned that:

1. The lists do not entirely correspond. This suggests that there is no exhaustive list, so we can never look at something which another Christian does for Christ and his Church and say that their ability is not a gift of the Holy Spirit.

2. The gifts are given not for personal glory or gain, but for the glory and honour of Christ and the strengthening of his Church.

3. Paul's picture of the Church as a body helps us to remember that we are all different, so we can expect to have different gifts. We should not necessarily seek what God has given to someone else.

4. The body works in harmony, with each part serving the good of the whole. This is a wonderful picture of the Church, each Christian using the gifts which God has given to him in a way which serves all the other believers. The gifts which the Holy Spirit gives to his Church are complementary, not in competition with each other.

5. If the Church is to be 'the Body of Christ' we need to identify the gifts which God has given to each believer and set them free to fulfil their own particular, distinctive ministry. If we do not, they are frustrated and every other Christian is impoverished. If we do, they are fulfilled and every other Christian is enriched.

*Take a moment to look around your group and identify the gifts which God has given to the other people present. Go round the group sharing what you have observed in each other (we are much better at seeing this in others than we are at seeing it in ourselves - so miss yourself out!). Affirm them and in your prayer time thank God for each other and the rich variety of gifts which he has given to even a small group like yours. It's all the Holy Spirit's work!*

# 5. What is the Church?

Let's begin by thinking of some of the ways in which the word 'church' is used today. Try to make up a few sentences using the word 'church'. Then ask yourselves what the word meant in each sentence. You may find it helpful to write the sentences down so that you don't forget them.

**Do this exercise now, before going any further with these notes!**

What have you learned? The word 'church' is used in a variety of different ways. Most often it refers to a building - *Altrincham Methodist Church*; sometimes it refers to a denomination - *The Methodist Church;* sometimes to Christians in a given place - *the church in Great Britain;* but the idea of the church as a building is probably the most common.

This is in sharp contrast to the biblical understanding of 'church'. In the pages of the New Testament the word 'church' is never used to refer to a building, because the first Christians didn't have any buildings which were devoted especially to Christian usage. In the New Testament the word 'church' always refers to people and never buildings.

The Greek word 'ekklesia' was used in secular Greek to describe a group of citizens who were gathered to discuss the affairs of state. It comes from two Greek words 'ek' meaning 'out of' and 'klesis' (from 'kaleo' - to call) meaning 'called'. The New Testament church was seen as a group of people who were called out of the world for a specific task. They were chosen people. They were called for a specific task; but most important of all the church was, and is, people!

Sometimes today you come across groups of Christians who attempt to preserve the distinction between buildings and people. Occasionally you see a notice board which says something like 'This is where the Stroud Baptist Church meets'. The early Methodists sought to preserve this distinction by calling their buildings 'chapels'. The chapel was where the church met.

Spend some time talking about the distinction between the church as a building and the church as people. Here are some questions to get you started:

- *How important are buildings to the church today?*
- *Do we spend too much time, effort and money maintaining church buildings?*
- *Does anyone in the group know of situations where a church has been established without the purchase of a building?*
- *Is it easier to sense that we really are church when we meet in places other than the church building?*

Wherever Christians gather - there is the church!

## *A Picture of the Church*

The New Testament gives us several different pictures of the church. Sometimes (as in Eph 2:19-22 and Peter 2:4) it is described as a 'living temple' with each member as a stone and all the stones together forming something which is built for the worship of God. Sometimes (as in Rev 21:2-3) it is described at 'the bride of Christ'. Here the emphasis is on a loving relationship between Christ and those he has chosen to be his own.

One of the most common pictures of the church is that of the body of Christ, where all the members are different parts of the one body, each fulfilling a different function, but together being Jesus in the world today.

This picture is used when Paul writes to the Church at Corinth. You can read about it in 1 Corinthians 12:12-27.

*Get one member of the group to read this passage now while everyone else follows in their own Bibles.*

What do we learn about the church from this picture? Note the following things:

1. There ought to be both a unity and a diversity about the church (12:12-13).

2. We all belong to Christ and to each other, so
   - We need each other (12:15,16,21)
   - We differ from each other (12:17-20)
   - We are to care for each other (12:22-26)
   - We are all individuals ( 12:27)

3. Try to relate these truths to your local church
   - *In what ways are our unity and our diversity demonstrated?*
   - *Does our church provide a genuine Christian welcome to a rich variety of people who may see things differently, but who are united in Christ?*
   - *Are there people who don't feel needed? How can we help them to feel that they really matter?*
   - *Is jealousy and rivalry a problem?*
   - *Are there those who see themselves as being more important than the rest? How can we help them to see their position in biblical terms, without making them feel unloved?*
   - *It is often easier to 'weep with those who weep' than to 'rejoice with those who rejoice'. How easy do we find it to be genuinely glad when others are blessed, used and praised?*
   - *How do we create the kind of atmosphere in which each person feels that they have a distinctive contribution to bring?*

## *The First Christians*

Read Acts 2:42-47. This is the earliest account we have of the first Christian church. Can you identify the things which were important for their life together and their spiritual growth? It is a wonderful picture of the way in which the first believers learned together, worshipped together, loved each other in practical ways and grew day by day. No one told them that this is how they ought to behave. It was the result of the Spirit's coming. The Holy Spirit transformed them and made this kind of community the 'natural' expression of their faith.

*What lessons do we need to learn from them?*

If that is what the Holy Spirit could do with such unlikely material there is hope for every Christian community when he comes among us.

# 6. The Life of Prayer

## What is Prayer?
There are many definitions of prayer. It is often called 'the breath of the soul'. It is a wonderful picture. The air which our body requires is all around us. It exerts pressure upon us and seeks to enter the body. That's why it is more difficult to hold your breath than to breathe. But as we allow the body to do what it was made to do, to breathe, the source of life enters us. Prayer, some have said, is like the breathing of the soul.

'To pray', said O Hallesby in his wonderful book *Prayer*, is 'to let Jesus come into our hearts...Prayer is an attitude of our hearts, an attitude of mind...an appeal to his heart.' Olive Wyon in her book *The School of Prayer* speaks of prayer as the 'lifting of heart and mind and will to God'.

Both these ways of looking at prayer focus our attention on something inside us. Prayer is not primarily concerned with external things like speech or silence, posture, or whether prayers are written or 'made-up'. Prayer is about an attitude, the direction which our lives are facing, a recognition of God and a longing for him.

*Take a moment to try to agree a definition of prayer in your group. Try not to concentrate on the things which prayer may involve (speech, silence, listening etc.) but rather on the heart of the matter. What is prayer?*

## The Example of Jesus
It is quite clear from the Gospels that the prayer life of Jesus made a profound impact on his disciples. He would often rise early for prayer, and get away from people to be alone with God (Matt 14:23, Mark 1:35, 6:46, Luke 5:16, 6:12). Sometimes, often after he had been pursued by a crowd of needy people, he would try and escape from them to pray alone (Mark 6:45-52). Prayer was the rhythm of his life.

It was quite natural, therefore, for his disciples to ask 'Lord, teach us to pray' (Luke 11:1). You will see from the context that their request was prompted by them seeing Jesus at prayer. There must have been a different quality about his prayer life. The disciples were all Jews and they would have been taught prayers from their childhood. In the temple and synagogue they would have seen many other people at prayer. But there was something distinctively different about the prayer life of Jesus. It was this distinctive quality which prompted their question.

**There is a world of difference between praying and saying prayers.**
*Spend a moment discussing what the difference is.*

The fact that Jesus responded to the disciples' request 'Lord, teach us to pray' indicates that he thought it was a reasonable question! He knew that prayer does not come naturally or easily even to people who were very close to him. We do not need to feel guilty about difficulties we have with prayer. Many Christians have problems with the life of prayer; but they are ashamed and afraid to admit it. They have been given the impression that it ought to come naturally, and so they are embarrassed about asking for help.

*In the confidence and security of your group try and be honest in acknowledging the difficulties which you have with prayer. Try to concentrate on your personal life of prayer rather than prayer in public worship. It may help you to make a list of the difficulties.*

*Now spend some time trying to help each other. What have you found helpful? How have you overcome some of the problems which have been mentioned? Share your positive experiences and try to learn from each other.*

## The Teaching of Jesus

Jesus tried to help his followers by his teaching as well as his example. Look at some of the Gospel passages which deal specifically with prayer. You will find some of them listed below. In each case try to sum up the central truth of the teaching in a short sentence. To frame the sentence '*This is teaching me........about prayer*' is a good way of doing it.

Matthew 6:5-15    Luke 11:1-13    Luke 18:1-14

The Matthew 6 and Luke 11 passages both include the prayer which Jesus gave to his followers, although the teaching which follows is different in each case.

Don't miss the opportunity of taking time to think about the Lord's Prayer. It is repeated so often in worship that many people don't think about what they are saying, so take some time to think about it now.

As well as being a prayer for us to repeat and make our own, the Lord's Prayer is a model for our own prayers. Take a look at the 'shape' of the prayer. Notice how it begins by concentrating on God and his glory, and only brings our need before him later. *Do we sometimes do things the other way round?* Notice that when human need is brought before God it is always in the plural - 'us' and 'our', not 'me' and 'mine'.

*What does this tell us about prayer?*

*Spend a moment or two sharing together some of the other things which the Lord's Prayer says to you about our own prayer life.*

## The Practice of Prayer

When it comes to the life of prayer we need more than an appreciation of its value. We can believe that prayer is a really good idea, and still not do much! It is precisely here that many Christians need help. For most of us the life of prayer presents three major challenges

## When do I pray?

Finding the time for prayer in a busy life can be very difficult. It is far more important that we spend time in prayer, than how much time we spend, or which part of the day we give to prayer.

Be realistic. Set yourself an achievable goal. If that's just five minutes each day, to start with, it's better than no time at all. Don't feel inadequate. The time will grow as prayer becomes an important feature of your walk with God.

Try not to leave God with the time of the day when you are at your worst. Some folk are morning people. Late at night is not their best time. Others come to life at the end of the day. Choose a time which is right for you, and stick to it. Try to see it as an appointment with God.

Our aim should be to have prayer as part of the rhythm of our day, just like cleaning our teeth. Occasionally we may not do it, but we quickly realize what we have missed!

*Share together the most suitable times of the day for members of your group,*

## Where do I pray?

In busy households finding the place for prayer can also be a problem. But Christians recognise that in a life-style where there are so many demands made upon us it is important to find a place where we can be alone with God.

To pray in bed, especially if lying down, is not the best place for many people. They seldom get to 'Amen'! Some people have a special place in their home, whilst others find that prayer comes easiest when walking the dog. There is no 'right' place for everyone; but it is important to find the right place for you.

*Share together the problems which you have encountered in trying to find a suitable place, and how you have overcome them.*

## How do I pray?

If prayer is about making contact with God we need to ask what helps us do that. For some people it is Christian music played on a tape or CD. Others find visual symbols helpful, a lighted candle or a devotional picture. Many Christians have linked their time of prayer with a short time of daily Bible study; reading the Bible not as a text book, but rather thinking themselves into the story and meeting God there.

*What do you find most helpful?*

Many Christians also find that the limited time they have available is best used if they plan their prayer time. They often follow the pattern which we have observed in the Lord's Prayer - acknowledging God's holiness, majesty and love before bringing their own needs and the needs of other before him. Some Christians keep a note of prayer requests which they plan systematically, say over a monthly period. Others follow a prayer manual in their prayers for others.

*Do you have a plan for your prayer time? What are the advantages and disadvantages of having a systematic plan?*

At the heart of prayer there lies a relationship with God. The life of prayer is about taking him into the reckoning in every area of our lives. Our aim is that prayer should become second nature. As we begin, like so many things, it demands some effort on our part; but the rewards are so great that they outweigh any cost which prayer involves.

Prayer changes people from the inside out - *and it can do so for you!*

# 7. What is Worship?

*Try to remember a service of worship which was really special for you, one in which you really encountered God. Share your memories with other members of your group. Now try to reflect on what made it special. Was it what was done? Was it the attitude of other people who were there? Was it the attitude in your own heart?*

Worship stands at the heart of the Christian faith. Being a Christian involves not only doing and believing the right things, but being in a relationship with God. The greatness, majesty and awesome power of God evoke within us a desire to worship him. He is altogether greater than we are. We come before him as creatures come before their creator.

The English word 'worship' comes from two Anglo-Saxon words which are best translated worth-ship. Worship involves acknowledging the worth of the One who is worshipped. Something of this comes through even in the secular use of the word. When someone thinks very highly of another we say 'He worships her' - he acknowledges her worth to him, to him she is very precious, and that attitude touches every aspect of their relationship.

We also need to remember that 'worship' is primarily a verb rather than a noun. Worship is something we do, not something we attend. We all know this to be true. We can attend worship, but never really worship. Just being there does not mean that we worship. To worship involves an attitude of the heart towards the One who is worshipped.

*Spend some time in your group trying to come to a definition, or at least an understanding, of worship. Share together, and try to complete the sentence 'Worship is...'*

## Worship in the Old Testament

*Take a look at some Old Testament passages which speak of people's attitude before God - Exodus 3:1-6, Isaiah 6:1-8, Psalm 8.*
*How would you describe the attitude of the people you have read about?*

The sense that God was altogether greater than human beings and required their worship posed a question for the worshipper: if God is so great and majestic, and if I am so small in comparison to him, how can I approach him at all?

The original Old Testament answer to this question was 'By way of sacrifice.' From the time of Abraham's call until the time of the exile worship involved sacrifice. It was through the offering of a life, or a portion of property, that men and women could approach God. This form of worship quickly became a system, administered by priests. When Solomon built his temple in Jerusalem it became the centre at which sacrifices were offered, and therefore the focus of worship for the Jewish nation. Before long the emphasis was placed on the outward form of worship, sacrifice, and not the attitude of the worshipper. Some of the prophets had some very strong things to say about this. Take a look at Micah 6:6-8.

*In what ways do you think that in our worship there is a danger of placing the emphasis on doing the right things rather than having the right attitude?*

It is only when we realise the extent to which Jerusalem had become the focus for worship that we begin to see what it meant for the Jewish nation to be taken into exile. In their minds, God was identified with a particular place and they were separated from that place by hundreds of miles when they were taken into exile in Babylon. Take a look at Psalm 137 to see how they felt - forsaken, alone and deprived of the central focus which their worship had always had.

*Do you think that something of this attitude is still with us? Do we associate worship with a particular place, building or form of service so that we cannot worship effectively without them? Is this one reason why some people find changes in worship so threatening?*

It was whilst the Jewish nation was in exile that the focus of worship changed from the sacrifices which were offered, to the Law which God had given. They no longer had the opportunity for sacrifice, but they still had the Law. It was a vital link with God and became the focus of all their worship. During this period worship practices grew up which eventually became a system of synagogues. The Law would be read and explained to the people and they would respond by living as God's Law required. Even when they returned to Jerusalem and the Temple was rebuilt they continued to worship in synagogues where the focus was on the Law. So, by the time of Jesus, the Jewish nation had two parallel forms of worship: the sacrificial system and the synagogue. It was against this background that Jesus ministered.

## Worship in the New Testament

Jesus clearly places the emphasis on the attitude of the one who worships and not on what the worshipper does. The Pharisees could not be faulted for their religious practices, but these were the very people against whom Jesus spoke most vigorously. Take a look, for example, at Luke 21:1-4. What does this tell us about the worship of the various people involved?

When Jesus spoke to a woman at a well (John 4) it was not long before they began to talk about worship. She was concerned to know about the acceptable practices (vv.19-20) but Jesus placed the emphasis not on what the worshipper did or where it was done, but on the attitude in the worshippers' heart (vv.21-24). For Jesus, if worship was to be genuine its primary concern was the heart of the worshipper reaching out to God and not the way the worshipper did it.

*Do you agree? How can we apply that truth today?*

Following the outpouring of the Holy Spirit at Pentecost worship became the central feature of the Christian's corporate and individual life. Look at Acts 2:42-47.

*What does this tell us about the worship of the first Christian community?*

It is clear that something wonderful had happened to them, something *inside* them, so that their hearts simply reached out in praise and worship to God. Worship was no longer a requirement laid upon them, but a spontaneous response to all that they had experienced. It was not an obligation but a privilege.

There are many other New Testament references to the worship of the Early Church. Paul had some very clear teaching about worship, especially when he wrote to the Church at Corinth. Yet, even though there were problems, it is clear that worship lay at the very centre of the church's life. To be a Christian was to be in a worshipping relationship with God.

*What have we learned so far about authentic Christian worship? Try to summarise the main points.*

## Worship Today

In our own generation worship has gone through many significant changes. There was a time when in Great Britain you could be quite sure what form the worship would take in any given church. It depended largely on the denomination. We used to know that Roman Catholics worshipped in a particular way, as did Anglicans, Methodists, Baptists, Salvation Army and so on. That has all changed. Within one denomination there are tremendous varieties of worship experiences on offer. When people move into a new area they no longer look for a church which is the same denomination as the one they have left, but for one where the worship which is offered, as well as other things, enables them to find God.

This means we must acknowledge that different people worship in different ways. Their tastes in worship are influenced by their background, temperament and Christian history. You often find that the worship experience through which someone came to faith has a formative effect on all their future worship patterns.

If the church is to meet the challenge of our generation it demands far more than tolerance from every Christian. Christians do not want to be tolerated in a local church, they want to be affirmed. If they feel that they are merely tolerated they will leave and find a church where they are affirmed.

*Is our church big enough to affirm positively those who may worship in ways which are quite different from our own?*

If the church is to enable a rich variety of people to find God it must take variety in worship seriously. We have a responsibility to provide a worshipping opportunity for all those whom God sends our way.

Worship would be revitalised if every member of the local church was there for every service. It would be dynamic if they all came expecting to meet with God.

*Is this too much to ask? How could we make progress towards that goal?*

# 8. Called as a Witness

'Witness' is a familiar word to everyone. We often encounter it in a legal setting. If legal documents like conveyances have to be drawn up they must be witnessed. The witness signs so that everyone concerned knows that the person required to sign (the owner of the property) actually did sign of their own free will, and the witness saw him do it. The other way in which many people are witnesses, is when they appear before a judge and jury in a court of law. Witnesses are required to give evidence about what they actually saw and heard. Honesty and impartiality are very important. To bear false witness is a criminal offence. Perjury is prohibited both in our own legal system and in biblical times (Ex 20:16; Deut 5:20).

*Has anyone in your group ever been called as a witness in a court of law? They could share the story, as far as they are able, with the whole group. How did they feel when they knew they were required to give evidence? How did they feel as they actually did so?*

## Christian Witness
### The Acts of the Apostles
According to St Luke the parting words of Jesus included both the command and the promise that his followers would be witnesses (Acts 1:8). The Greek word for witness is *martureo* from which we get the word 'martyr'. It reminds us clearly of the lengths to which they were willing to go as they bore their witness to Christ. Many of them would rather die than deny that which they knew to be true.

To what could the first followers of Jesus bear witness? It was simply what they had seen and heard. They could not stop talking about it, despite all the threats they received (Acts 4:20). Yet, as they began to tell their story they made it clear that it was not just an account of a person that they had known and loved. They also stated their conviction that in a unique way God was involved in the life, ministry, death and resurrection of Jesus. They told the historic story, but interpreted it in such a way that the hearers understood the story to be revealing God's plan, purposes and offer to all mankind. Take a look at part of Peter's sermon on the Feast of Pentecost (Acts 2:22-24) or Paul's way of interpreting the central facts of the Christian story (1 Cor 15:1-8; 2 Cor 5:19-20).

An even closer examination of the Acts of the Apostles reveals more about the content of their witness. We discover that out of the thirteen times the noun 'witness' is used two of them are not specifically Christian (Acts 6:13, 7:58). The remaining eleven are very interesting. Look them up in the order in which they occur - Acts 1:8, 1:22, 2:32, 5:32, 10:39, 10:41, 13:31, 22:15, 22:20 and 26:16.

*From your examination of these verses, what were the early Christians witnesses to?*

Of these eleven verses only one has nothing to do with the resurrection (10:39). Of the other ten, five are concerned exclusively with it, and the other five include reference to the resurrection when we study the contexts in which they were given.

The Early Church wanted, above everything else, to make it known that the resurrection had happened and that Jesus was alive. They were not living on their recollections of a dead teacher, however great. They were joyful and confident servants of a living Lord. They were not concerned about vague hopes, but about the historic fact of the resurrection and the difference which this had made to their own lives.

*Why do you think that the resurrection was such an important feature of their witness?*

## Bearing Witness Today

Modern Christians cannot, of course, bear witness to the life, death and resurrection of Jesus in precisely the same way as the apostles did because they did not meet him physically, hear his teaching, see his death or witness his resurrection. Christians today can simply repeat the witness of the apostles which is recorded in the Bible. However, there is one important addition to the apostolic witness which modern Christians can bring. They can testify that they have proved this to be true by their own experience. It is this authentic testimony which makes the gospel sound immediate and convincing for people today. We take notice when someone says 'I have tried this and it worked for me'.

Bearing all this in mind there are some important lessons to be learned from the New Testament which can make our witness today so much more effective. Take some time to consider each of these observations and discuss the questions which follow each one:

1. The New Testament Christians witnessed by what they were as well as by what they said. They were living advertisements for the gospel they proclaimed. It really had made a difference to their lives. What we say is useless if it is not endorsed by a quality of living which is clearly evident. To proclaim a truth and live as though it were not true is a contradiction which the world sees as hypocrisy.

*Is there enough difference between the life-style of Christians and non-Christians in the modern western world? In what ways should Christians stand out from the rest of society?*

2. The gospel needs also to be shared in words as well as deeds. If people are to believe in Jesus they need to know what the central Christian message is. Explanation is necessary. Like Peter and Paul we need to be able to interpret history in a way which impacts the lives of the hearers.

*Imagine that you have just met a stranger on a bus or train, who is really anxious to know what it is to be a Christian. They get off at the next stop. You have just a few minutes to share the heart of the Christian faith with them. What would you say?*

3. The resurrection either happened or it did not. It is either true or false. It cannot be true for me because I choose to believe it and false for you because you choose to deny it. If we are to be as effective in our witness as the early Christians were we need to be as convinced as they were about the truth of the resurrection.

*How convinced are you that Jesus rose from the dead? Honestly share both your doubts and your certainties.*

4. The first Christians spoke of the gospel making a difference to their own lives. It was not a theory to be accepted but an offer to be received. They were preoccupied with the impact Jesus had made to them and the difference he could make to the lives of their hearers.

*In a short sentence, and avoiding Christian 'jargon', try to sum up the difference which Jesus has made to you.*

## Telling your Story

Many Christians find that when the opportunity to witness for Christ presents itself they are lost for words. When the opportunity has gone they think what they ought to have said! This indicates that we all need to have something clearly worked out in our minds which we are ready to share when we are given the chance to do so. This is best done first amongst other Christians where we feel secure and valued. To share our story in such a group strengthens us and encourages others.

There are a number of classic ways of giving a testimony. Here is one:

- What was life like **before** you became a Christian?
- **How** did you become a Christian?
- What **difference** has it made being a Christian?

*Can you think about your own Christian journey in this way? Share your stories in the group.*

Another way is to speak of some aspect of the Christian life which has really been valuable to you. This is especially worthwhile if it resonates with the hearer in a personal way.

- You may speak about **a crisis** in which your faith made a real difference.
- It may be **a quality** of life you have found - a sense of purpose, peace or joy.
- It may be the strength you have found, enabling you to cope with **a difficulty**.

Often people who have grown up in the church, and who cannot remember a time when they were not Christian, find this the easiest way.

*Think about some area in your life where being a Christian has made a real difference and, amongst your friends in the group, share your story.*

Very often the world is more ready to hear than we are to tell. Try to work out now what you would say if you had the chance, so that you are ready when the opportunity comes along - as it surely will!

# 9. Life in the Spirit

## How is it for you?
Some people find the Christian life very hard. It seems to be a great struggle. Begin this session by thinking about how easy or hard you find the Christian life yourself. Think about your own Christian life and give yourself a score on a scale of 1-10 where 1 is very easy and 10 is extremely hard. Each person should do this exercise on their own first, and then when everyone has done it share your findings.

*Do this now before you proceed with the rest of this study.*

## Should it be like this?
Sometimes we meet other Christians whose lives really impress us. For them things seem to be different. The Christian life does not seem to be a struggle for them, endlessly trying to keep almost impossible standards. They seem to have an inner power, a new dynamic, which makes such a difference. They may not say anything to us, but the quality of their lives reminds us that there must be a better way. They seem to have discovered a secret which we do not know.

*Take a moment for different people in your group to share stories about the Christians that they have known who are like this.*

## What's the secret?
From a human point of view the Christian life is not difficult, it's impossible! It's not just a matter of living by a new set of standards. It's also about the inward things - our thoughts, attitudes, motives and intentions. To get those right, as well as to live according to the standards of the Kingdom of God, is quite impossible for a normal human being.

But God would never invite us into a new life if it were impossible for us. The very fact that the Christian life is offered to us suggests that there must also be some resources offered that enable us to live this kind of life.

Most people who find the Christian life very hard begin by assuming that success or failure depends on them. The emphasis is on what *they* do. But the people who seem to have discovered the secret put the emphasis in a different place. It is not about what *they* do, but about what *God does* in them. This new awareness gives them the clue which makes all the difference. Success or failure does not now depend on their effort but on their willingness to allow God to do his work in and through them. That is why they are reluctant to accept praise or even appreciation. They know that the credit is not down to them. Anything that has been achieved has not been because of them. It has been because God did it, in them and through them.

Another way of looking at this question is to recognise the distinction between what God does *for* us and what he does *in* us. In so many ways, but supremely in the life, death and resurrection of Jesus, God does so much for us. In fact he does everything necessary for us to begin a new life! But if we stop there we only have half a gospel. The other half is about what he does *in* us.

When we become Christians the Holy Spirit comes to live in our lives. He brings all the resources which God can provide to enable us to live the kind of life which he wants. This new quality of living is dependent not on our effort, but on his power at work within our lives, to his glory.

Christian writers use different phrases to describe this quality of Christian living. Some call it 'the higher life', others 'life in Christ', others 'the Spirit-filled life', others 'life in the Spirit'. The phrases they use may be different, but they are all describing a quality of Christian living which is made possible not by the effort of the individual Christian, but by what God's Spirit is doing within them.

*Take a moment to share together how you feel about what you have just read. Has this come as a new insight, or a repetition of a familiar truth? Share your reflections before moving on to think about what the Bible says.*

## The Early Church

Even after the resurrection of Jesus the disciples were still very confused. They had followed Jesus, witnessed his death and even met him as a Risen Lord; but that did not solve all their problems or give their lives a new direction. When Peter said 'I'm going fishing' (John 21:3) it spoke volumes about his attitude. He was returning to the life he had known before. The other disciples agreed to go with him, for they too lacked any sense of new direction in their lives. Even after the death and resurrection of Jesus there was still something missing.

The coming of the Holy Spirit at Pentecost changed all that. To compare Peter before and after Pentecost is to recognise the transformation which had taken place. The one who was disillusioned became the one who stood and proclaimed Christ fearlessly to the waiting crowd. The difference came about because he, and the other disciples, were 'filled with the Holy Spirit' (Acts 2:4).

It is clear that the leaders of the Early Church recognised the crucial importance of the Holy Spirit in the life of every Christian. So much so that even when they heard about people becoming Christians they were anxious to make sure that they knew the dynamic power of the Holy Spirit before they went forward into their new life.

*Read Acts 8:4-17 as an example of this.*
Peter and John went from Jerusalem to Samaria to make sure that those who had become Christians there knew the inner resources of the Holy Spirit for their new Christian life.

We have a similar situation in Acts 18 and 19. Paul had visited Ephesus once, but had to leave before his task was completed. Apollos took over, but when

Paul arrived back there he saw that there was something missing from the lives of those who had responded to Apollos' message.
*Read Acts 18:24-19:7*
Paul was quick to identify their deficiency. They lacked the dynamic of the Holy Spirit, and Paul was anxious to put the matter right straight away.

In both these cases people had made a commitment to Christ before they knew the dynamic transformation which is brought about by the coming of the Holy Spirit in a personal way. It is important to notice that this pattern is not repeated in every case of people becoming Christians in the Acts of the Apostles. In some the Holy Spirit is never mentioned. However, it is clear that in cases such as the Ethiopian official (Acts 8) or the Philippian Jailer (Acts 16) there was a new quality of life which was evident to others. It is this new quality of living which the apostles are anxious to ensure is present in every Christian. In Acts the emphasis clearly rests on the quality of life evident in each Christian, rather than the number of spiritual experiences which each Christian has had.

## The good can be the enemy of the best
Paul often describes two ways of living. He holds them before his readers, so that they can see the contrast. These are not the life of the non-Christian and the life of the Christian. Both can be Christians, but one has discovered the new dynamic which the Spirit is able to give. Take a look at two examples:

*Romans 7:21-8:8*
*In verses 21-25 Paul describes one kind of life, and in 8:1-8 he describes the other. Read these two passages one after the other. It may be best if a different person in the group reads each one. Ask yourself which one best describes your experience.*

*Galatians 5:16-26*
It is clear from vv.16-18 that Paul is aware of the inner conflict which many Christians face. In vv.19-21 he describes human nature and in vv.22-26 he describes the character of the Spirit-filled life.
*Once again, read this passage. It may be best if one person reads vv.16-18 as the introductory paragraph, another vv.19-21 and another vv.22-26. Do you recognise the tension of which Paul speaks? With which of the last two paragraphs do you most closely identify?*

Every Christian ought to know the kind of life which is offered through the indwelling Holy Spirit. It is a complete inward transformation, enabling us to live the kind of life which God requires. But how can this be mine?

## The way in
We were never intended to live the Christian life in our own strength. The trouble is that we keep trying! It is only when we realise our utter helplessness

that God is able to step in and fill us with his Spirit. This is in such contrast to the world's standards. For the Christian, the key to strength is in admitting our weakness and opening our lives to all that God can do.

*Read John 12:23-26*
This is not just describing what is going to happen to Jesus. He is giving us an insight into a spiritual law. It is by dying that we live. By making ourselves nothing we can become all that God can make us.

*Read Luke 11:11-13*
God is not reluctant to fill us with his Spirit. We must realise our own inability and ask him to fill us with his Spirit. That is all.

**God always has more for those who are prepared to receive what he wants to give. Has he spoken to you in this session? What do you need to do?**

# 10. Called to Simplicity

Most of us enjoy a higher standard of living than we have ever known before. We expect that it should get higher with every passing year. We are more affluent than we have ever been.

*Take five minutes to make a list of the things which we now enjoy which were not available to ordinary people in our childhood.*

For Christians who seek to walk close to the Lord this can create real tensions. On the one hand we enjoy the easier life-style which modern conveniences provide. On the other hand we feel uneasy about some biblical teaching on possessions and we cannot avoid the contrast between our own life-style and the abject poverty in which so many of the world's population live.

The call to a simple life-style, which is an unavoidable part of the gospel, is a call to *choose* to live simply as a testimony to the transient nature of wealth and the love of God for everyone. If God loves each person equally, surely they should all have a fair share of the resources available and have equal opportunities.

For modern, western, comfortable Christians the biblical teaching on simplicity can be very hard. Maybe that is why so many ignore it, rationalize their own position with heretical prosperity doctrines or develop a distorted view that God has particularly chosen and blessed them whilst ignoring the poverty of so many. We need to take a closer look at what the Bible says.

## The Old Testament

Even though Christians may understand the creation stories (Genesis 1-3) in different ways the truth which they contain cannot be ignored. They have much to teach us about God as the Creator of everything, about human beings being made in his image and about the human race being entrusted with God's creation. Human beings are given the responsibility of looking after God's creation for him. They do not own it and they should never count it theirs.

As God's people developed in their understanding of God and their relationship with him, stress was laid on their responsibility for the land and all that the land produced, for that was where their wealth lay. It was considered threatening to their relationship with God if they considered anything *their* possession. Read Lev 25:23 to see how this view was reflected in the Old Testament law. Because the earth belongs to the Lord none of it could be held perpetually.

The Old Testament writers knew how easy it is to trust one's possessions instead of trusting God. The Psalmist identifies this danger in Psalm 62:10. To trust one's possessions was seen as undermining the people's relationship with God. The Old Testament prophets constantly denounced the acquisition of wealth, especially if it was done at the expense of the poor. For one person to have more than their rightful share meant that others had less than their rightful share. Take a look at Amos 4:1ff and Isa 3:13-15 as good examples of this.

There is no doubt that, when taken as a whole, the Old Testament sees wealth and possessions as both a privilege and a danger. We are privileged that God has entrusted the whole of creation to us, but we are in danger of placing our reliance on things rather than on him. This creates a fundamental change in the kind of relationship which God desires with his people.

## The New Testament

Christians are followers of One who was born in poverty and raised in obscurity. There is no record of him owning anything except the robe which he wore at the crucifixion. He was buried in a borrowed tomb. He viewed possessions with considerable suspicion, was completely free from the cares which they bring, lived in daily dependence on his heavenly Father and taught his followers to do the same.

*Take a look at Matthew 6:24-34 and Luke 12:16-21.*
*What do both these passages tell us about Jesus' view of possessions? What teaching do they contain for Jesus' followers?*

It is no accident that the first Christian community of which we have a record took a very light view of possessions. Acts 2:43-44 records their attitude. It was a natural expression of what had happened to them at Pentecost. There had been a fundamental change in their priorities.

*Take a look at Acts 4:32-37. What does this tell us about the early Christians' attitude to possessions? What kind of a witness do you think this made in a greedy, acquisitive world?*

*You may also want to look at 1 Tim 6:9, James 4:1&2 and Phil 4:12&19. What do we learn from each of these texts about possessions and the dangers which they can bring to our spiritual lives?*

## Christians down the ages

From the earliest days of the Christian Church there have been those within it who have realized how seductive possessions can be. Because they have been very serious about their quest for a deeper relationship with God they have renounced wealth and possessions. This emphasis has manifested itself in a variety of ways, depending on the branch of the Church to which these Christians have belonged. For some it has meant the complete renunciation demanded by the monastery. For others it has been the renunciation which particular areas of Christian service demand.

For many in the Puritan or Evangelical tradition it has not meant leaving the 'world' with its possessions, but adopting a completely different attitude towards them. Often the things which the world prizes most highly, like money and appearance, have been dismissed as inconsequential. Wesley told his sister, 'Money never stays with me. It would burn me if it did. I throw it out of my hands as soon as possible, lest it should find its way into my heart'. He told everyone that if at his death he was found with more than ten pounds in his possession, people would have the privilege of calling him a robber. Near the end of his life he wrote in his Journal, 'I left no money in my will, because I have none'.

In our own generation many Christians, particularly in Latin America and the Third World, have reminded us that sin is not just an individual matter. We are called to struggle against sinful economic systems which oppress the poor so that the rich can live in luxury. Several, like Oscar Romero, have been martyred as a consequence.

## Being a Christian in the Modern World

In a world of complicated economic systems like ours it is virtually impossible for an individual to be squeaky-clean if they have any money or possessions at all. Most of us have no idea where our money is invested or what it is used for. But that does not mean that we should not try to live as near to the pattern of Jesus as possible.

To maintain a healthy detachment from 'things' is a great witness in a world where so many lives are dominated by possessions. Christians know that they do not need to earn acceptance by dressing in the right way or adopting a particular life-style. Real love, the love of God, is offered not because of what we are, but despite what we are. Possessions do not make a statement about an individual's worth.

We often have to say 'No' to something in order to say 'Yes' to something else. In every generation those who have renounced possessions remind us that being free from them enables us to be free for God and his purposes in our lives. The world often could not understand them, but they had what really matters.

We all have too many 'things'. We think they make life easier. In fact they make it harder, because each new possession brings its own list of worries. The simplicity teaching of the Bible, the example of Jesus and the model of the Early Church offer a radical alternative for Christians, even in the 21st century.

Here is one way of understanding the Christian attitude to possessions:

When we become Christians we are called to offer everything to Christ. That includes all that we own. There can be no half-hearted commitment. In practice this may take some time in the life of an individual Christian. Gradually we are brought to the point of surrendering everything to our Master. In his love, God then gives these things back to us. But this time we do not own them; we serve as stewards of them on his behalf. This means that our possessions are only ours until someone else needs them. When that happens the Christian offers whatever he can in the service of his Lord. His first question is always 'Lord, what would you have me to do?'

*Do you think this is an acceptable way of understanding our discipleship? How practical is it? Share together ways in which members of your group try to express Christian simplicity in their lifestyles?*

# 11. Jesus' Attitude to Others

The personality of Jesus constantly challenges both the individual Christian and the Church. He is the model for the attitude and behaviour of all his followers. The Church is the Body of Christ. As such it must represent Jesus in the world today. The Church's attitude should be the same as that of its Lord.

In this study we are going to examine the way Jesus saw his own ministry and the way in which this was demonstrated in his attitude to those he encountered. We should expect to be challenged as we remember that he is our model.

## How did Jesus see His own Ministry?

### 1. The Servant
Supremely, Jesus came to live as a servant. Rather than keep power exclusively for himself, he came to offer it to others (Mk10:45)
- In his death Jesus fulfilled Isaiah's prophecy concerning God's suffering servant (Isa 52:13-53:12).
- In his life he demonstrated unparalleled humility and gentleness. John the Baptist assumed the place of the second lowest servant in a household by denying his worthiness to even remove the shoes of Jesus (John 1:27). But Jesus took for himself the role of the lowest slave in actually washing the feet of his disciples. Jesus demonstrated this quality of servanthood in every part of his life.

*Take a moment to reflect together on the servanthood of Christ. How amazing is the grace of God, that the Lord of heaven and earth should choose the role of a servant. It may help you to read what Paul says about it in Phil 2:1-11 where it is seen as the pattern for Christian behaviour. What does this say to Christians who value their status or place great store on what others think about them? What does it say about churches which place so much emphasis on their size and reputation? How is this challenging you?*

### 2. The Friend
- Jesus showed affection and felt deep emotion in dealings with his friends, like the family at Bethany (John 11:33-38).
- Jesus received gifts with courtesy (John 12:7-8).
- Jesus was capable of relaxing when in the company of those whose friendship he appreciated (John 12:2).
- Jesus received verbal abuse for being the friend of tax collectors and sinners (Matt 11:19).
- Even though he was the Son of God there was nothing distant or aloof about Jesus. He was a friend to all who opened their lives to him, especially those who knew the rejection of others. He spoke with great authority and ministered with great power, yet was always approachable.

*How does the church sometimes give the impression that Jesus is remote from ordinary people? In what ways do we need to change so that we might offer the friendship of Jesus to those around us? Who ought we to be befriending for Jesus sake? How does the friendliness of Jesus challenge our attitude to those outside the Church?*

**The attitude of Jesus**

The way Jesus saw his ministry, as servant and friend, is demonstrated in his attitude to other people. Or to put it the other way round, his attitude to others indicates how he saw his ministry. How *did* Jesus relate to those around him, especially the disadvantaged? We shall think about several such groups.

○ **To Women**

Women were among the social outcasts of the time. Each morning a Pharisee rose to thank God that he was not born 'a Gentile, a slave or a woman' in that order! Yet it was precisely in that culture that Jesus gave dignity and significance to women.

- Jesus numbered many women among his friends (John 12:1-8), even 'fallen women' like Mary Magdalene and others (Matt 26:7, Mk 8:2, Lk 7:39, 8:1-3).
- Jesus healed the diseases of women (Mk 5:25, Matt 9:20).
- Jesus forgave the woman caught in adultery (John 8:3-11).
- Jesus chose an immoral woman to tell her village about him (John 4:3-42).
- It was women who mourned his arrest (Lk 23:27).
- A group of women travelled from Galilee to minister to his needs as he died (Matt 27:55).
- His first appearance after his resurrection was to a woman (John 20:15).
- Knowing the casual way men were treating divorce, which condemned women to a life of poverty, he spoke out (Matt 5:31-32, Mk 10:2-9).
- He was swift to challenge and rebuke male lust (Matt 5:28).

○ **To Children**

Unlike normal Jewish practice of his day, Jesus always seemed to have a special place in his heart for children:

- When people brought children to Jesus he rebuked the disciples for trying to turn them away (Mk 10:13-16).
- Jesus used a child as an example (Matt 18:2) and declared that a childlike spirit was essential to enter the kingdom (Matt 18:3-4).
- Jesus commanded that children be well received (Mk 9:37).
- Jesus warned against doing anything which caused a child to stumble (Lk 17:2).

○ **To His Family**

It cannot have been easy to be a relation of Jesus. He saw his family in broader terms than a part-shared physical relationship (Matt 12:48-50):

- Originally his brothers did not believe in him (Jn 7:5), but James, the eldest, eventually joined his disciples (Acts 1:14) and later became the leader of the church in Jerusalem (Acts 15:13, 21:18).
- Mary, his mother, spent time after the birth of Jesus considering all that had happened (Lk 2:19). Jesus after his visit to the Temple at the age of

12, again caused her to think - although she did not yet understand (Lk 2:50-51).
- Mary's lack of understanding continued at the wedding feast in Cana of Galilee; but by this time she knew enough to instruct the servants 'Do whatever he tells you' (Jn 2:5).
- Later his actions caused his family to question his sanity (Mk 3:21). But Mary was at the cross looking at her Son as he suffered (Jn 19:25). Jesus saw her and was careful to provide in the disciple he loved and valued someone who would look after her in the future (Jn 19:26-27).

○ **To The Foreigner**
Jesus crossed all boundaries of race and culture. Whilst he acknowledged the special status of Israel and God's chosen people (Matt 10:5&6) and made his appeal primarily to them, he was not exclusive in this (Lk 6:17):
- He applauded the faith of a Roman military officer (Mt. 8:10).
- He was prepared to help a Syro-Phoenician (Mt. 15:28).
- While Jesus was a boy the Samaritans had desecrated the Jerusalem Temple, scattering human bones in it during the Passover, but Jesus was prepared to spend time in Samaria.
- Despite antagonism towards him he refused his disciples' suggestion of retaliation against Samaritans (Lk 9:51-56).
- Normally a self-respecting Jew would make a 50-mile detour to avoid travelling through Samaria. John records that Jesus 'had to go through Samaria' (Jn 4:4).
- This led to a Samaritan woman being transformed and her witness attracting the whole village to Jesus. As a result, for the first time, he was acknowledged as 'the Saviour of the world' (Jn 4:42), and not merely the Messiah of the Jews.

○ **To Outcasts**
Jesus was concerned for those shunned by the rest of society:
- He saved the life of a woman caught in the act of adultery (Jn 8:1-11).
- To a tax collector (a collaborator with the occupying forces) he brought personal salvation and a deep desire to make proper restitution (Lk 19:1-10).
- The thief on the cross was given the assurance of Paradise (Lk 23:43).
- A sinful woman who anointed his feet received forgiveness (Lk 7:48).

During this study you may have been able to identify some of the groups mentioned with similar groups in our own society. Far from conforming to the cultural norms of his own generation, Jesus challenged them both in his teaching and his behaviour. He would simply do anything to demonstrate that God's love was for everyone. There was a place for everyone in his kingdom.

*In the light of this study take a moment to think of groups or subcultures with whom Jesus would especially identify today. How can we, as individuals and as a church, offer the love and friendship of Jesus to them?*

# 12. Jesus and His Enemies

In our last study we considered how Jesus saw his own ministry and how that shaped his attitude to others. We considered especially his attitude to groups who were marginalised within his society: women, children and outcasts.

But those were not the only people Jesus encountered. He also had his enemies. In this study we will think about two particular groups, the Pharisees and the Sadducees. They were his enemies because he was so outspoken against them and their opposition eventually led to the conspiracy which resulted in his death. But who were they and why was Jesus so outspoken against them?

*Take a moment to share together what you already know about the Pharisees and Sadducees. Try to describe their views and the influence which they had on society. Do not cheat by looking at the rest of these notes!*

What many people do not realize is that the Pharisees and Sadducees were strongly opposed to each other. Yet both these groups were so opposed to Jesus that they seem to have called a truce (John 11:47; Matt 16:1) and joined forces to oppose him. It says much about the threat which Jesus brought to them when we remember that even the occupying Roman forces had failed to make them do this.

Before we think about each group in detail we also need to remember that as God's Servant Jesus flatly refused to tell people what they wanted to hear. It is clearly demonstrated in his dealings with the religious leaders of his day.

## The Sadducees
These were primarily political figures in Jewish affairs:
- They provided the majority of the 70 elders in the Jewish Sanhedrin, the supreme court of the Jewish nation. Consequently they were in control of internal affairs, though subject to the Roman governor. In practice Rome used to let her colonies look after their own internal administration, providing it did not cause problems.
- Most of the Sadducees came from wealthy, aristocratic families. Josephus, a contemporary Jewish historian says of them, 'They only gain the well-to-do; they have not the people on their side'. The High Priest and Temple officials were usually drawn from this group. Some scholars believe that their name and origin are derived from Zadok, the High Priest during David's reign (2 Sam 8:17). They held a position of power and control in the religious life of the nation.
- They rejected most of the supernatural elements of the Jewish faith, including belief in angels, the spirit and the resurrection of the dead.
- Unlike the Pharisees they held only the written Law and rejected any consequential additions which men had imposed. In other words, they believed that the written word alone was the seat of religious authority.

- They also differed from the Pharisees in that they virtually rejected any sense of God controlling the affairs of men. Man's destiny, they believed, lay entirely in his own hands. They felt no need for divine providence to order their lives.
- Here we have a group of religious aristocrats who maintained control both of secular internal affairs and religious worship. Yet they had rationalized their faith, denying the supernatural and placing man's destiny in his own hands.
- They turned the Temple, 'the house of prayer', into a money-making opportunity.
- They turned devotion to God into a stifling legalism which preserved their power and control.

Can you think of a similar group, either in history or in our own day, in society or the church?

While Jesus denounced the Sadducees as a party, he did not criticise the institution of the priesthood itself. He did not confuse the system with the corruption of the system.
- Jesus scorned the disbelief of the Sadducees on the issue of resurrection (Mk 12:18-27), and warned the people against them (Matt 16:6). He accused them of neither knowing the scriptures nor the power of God (Matt 22:29).
- It is worth remembering that even though the Early Church suffered persecution at the hands of the Sanhedrin and the Jewish authorities (Acts 4:1, 5:17, 24:1-25:3), a 'large number of priests' became followers of Jesus (Acts 6:7).

## The Pharisees

The Pharisees emerged as a reforming movement during the second century BC. There were about 6,000 Pharisees at the time of Jesus.
- They aimed to draw the Jews back into a proper relationship with God, so concentrated their efforts on a scrupulous observance of the Jewish Law and could not conceive of anyone who did not keep the Law in every detail having a relationship with God.
- The majority of the scribes, the professional teachers and students of scripture, belonged to one or other of the Pharisaic groups.
- They taught the 'traditions of the elders' which meant the hundreds of laws and sub-laws which they devised in order to meet the standards laid down in the written Law.
- Their rigid observance of laws of ritual purity and tithing made it extremely difficult for them to eat a meal with anyone outside their own group. They were virtually an exclusive group. One group of the Pharisees would not even look at a Gentile.

- All these things moulded the way they saw themselves, as the only correct ones, and the way they saw others, as sinners. They were very sure of their own standing with the Almighty and held others in contempt.
- They placed all the emphasis on external religious practices. Jesus, in contrast, spoke of God being more concerned with the motive, the heart of people.

*Again, try to think of another group, in history or today, who are like the Pharisees in some respect.*

Jesus was totally uncompromising in his condemnation of the legalism of the Pharisees (Matt 15:1-11). He saw through external appearances (Matt 23:27-28) and warned that unless people's righteousness was greater than that of the Pharisees they would never enter the Kingdom of God (Matt 5:20).

When Jesus denounced the religious leaders of the day it was only because he knew their true motivation. But when he recognised spiritual hunger in a leading Pharisee, Nicodemus, he pointed him to the need for a fresh start, a new birth.

*Pause for a moment. What have you learned so far about the dangers of corruption and legalism, about God's requirements, about Jesus' reaction, about yourself?*

### Jesus' Response

Jesus taught his followers to love their enemies, and he did so himself. But he hated the self-righteousness, the corruption, the twisted motives and the legalism which ground others down and maintained status for a few. He knew what the consequences would be, but he never flinched from speaking out against evil and corruption wherever he saw it, even though it made him unpopular.

This raises lots of questions for Christians today. You may want to talk about them:

1. Do you think we sometimes, either as individuals or as a church, tone down our condemnation of evil because we think that to speak out would make us unpopular?
2. Why do we find it so difficult to 'love the sinner but hate the sin'? How can we distinguish, as Jesus did, between the individual and the views they hold or the things they are involved in?
3. What are the particular evils today against which we should speak out if we had the guts and didn't mind losing face?
4. Can you think of situations in which we ourselves might be accused of adopting a 'pharisaic' attitude?

# HEADWAY

A movement of Methodists committed to prayer for revival and witness to the evangelical faith.

The aims of the movement are...

- The promotion of the renewal and revival of the work, worship, and witness of the Church, particularly within Methodism, through prayer and in the power of the Holy Spirit.
- The encouragement of prayer for revival at a personal level, and in the church at home and overseas.
- The furtherance of informed theological discussion in the Church.
- The furtherance of thinking and action on ethical and social issues in a responsible and compassionate way, based on the belief that the righteous will of God must be expressed in the life of society.
- The promotion of joint action with evangelical Christians in all denominations of the Church in local and national events.
- The promotion of mature Christian spirituality in the lives of all members of the Church.

Our basis of faith is that of the Evangelical Alliance, with a specific commitment to the Methodist understanding of salvation, as set out in the FOUR ALLS.
- All people need to be saved
- All people can be saved
- All people can know themselves to be saved
- All people can be saved to the uttermost

Membership of HEADWAY is open to any member of the Methodist Church who is in sympathy with the aims and basis of the movement. Associate membership is open to those who are not members of the Methodist Church. Further information from the Membership Secretary

Find us at: www.methodistevangelicals.org.uk
*or write to us*
c/o **Moorleys Print & Publishing Ltd.,**
**23 Park Road, Ilkeston, Derbyshire DE7 5DA**
*who will pass on your valued enquiry.*